SOUTH-EAST ENGLAND fron
(Surrey, Sussex and Kent)

CONTENTS

Dover harbour front cover
Wye Crown back cover

Kent
Chatham Harbour 2
Upnor Castle 2
Chatham Historic Harbour 3
Rochester 3
Leeds Castle 4
Wye Crown 4
Boxley & The Pilgrim's Way 5
Canterbury Cathedral 5
Richborough Castle 6
Walmer Castle 6
Hever Castle 7
Chartwell 7
Knole House 8
Biggin Hill 8
Brands Hatch 9
Dungeness 9
Ramsgate 10
Broadstairs 10
Foreness Point 11
Margate 11
Dover Castle 12
White Cliffs of Dover 12
Channel Tunnel Terminal 13
Castle Hill Fort 13
Saltwood Castle 14
English Channel 15

West Sussex
Arundel Castle 16
Bodiam Castle 17
Selsey Bill 18
Bognor Regis 18
Chichester Harbour 19

East Sussex
Newhaven 19
Brighton 20
White Cliffs 21
Beachy Head 21
Caburn Hill Fort 22
Long Man of Wilmington 23
Bewl Water and Weald 24
Hastings 24
Battle Abbey 25

Surrey
M25/M23 junction 26
Epsom Race Course 27
Woodcote Park 27
New Malden & A3 28
Shere 28
Boxhill 29
Dorking 29
Guildford 30
Compton 30
Farnham Castle 31
Newark Priory 31

INTRODUCTION

Sussex, Surrey and Kent form the south-eastern corner of Britain, the region most heavily influenced by neighbouring continental Europe throughout its history. The south-east is a gentle landscape of fields and woodlands, the rolling North and South Downs and the Weald. To the north are the River Thames and London, and to the south the English Channel, one of the busiest waterways in the world.

The chalk downs are scattered with the remains of Iron Age hill fort settlements. The chalk proved ideal ground for the carving of hill figures, such as the Long Man of Wilmington. The Pilgrim's Way, an ancient route for pilgrims travelling from Winchester to Canterbury, follows the line of the North Downs. The famous white chalk cliffs along the south-east coast have been a welcoming sight for countless homeward bound travellers and indeed sailors, soldiers and airmen in times of war.

Today, the affluence of the south east is due to its proximity to London, to the Continent, and to the major airports at Heathrow and Gatwick, attracting the wealthy and the successful to build large properties hidden along leafy lanes. As London continues to expand, encircled by the M25 with its steady stream of traffic, it has swallowed up many quaint villages. Many have grown into towns to accommodate homes for London's workers and all the infrastructure required for the growth in population.

You will still find beautiful landscapes. Kent is often called the Garden of England – it is a county famous for its hop fields and orchards and its distinctive coastline. Surrey is one of the smallest English counties, and lies on the fringes of the ever expanding capital. Sussex has Brighton, beaches and Bognor Regis, apparently the sunniest place in England; castles, cliffs and enigmatic chalk hill figures. Throughout the south-east are patchworks of fields, woodland, and glimpses of the ancient past.

Photographs from top to bottom: M25/M23 junction, Walmer Castle, fog on the South Downs, white cliffs near Beachy Head

Photographs, text and design by Adrian Warren and Dae Sasitorn

MYRIAD BOOKS LIMITED

CHATHAM HARBOUR, Kent (above)

The importance of Chatham lies in its position on the Medway estuary. Back in the 16th century, Henry VIII's navy found that the peninsular now covered by dockyards was an ideal site for refitting ships with its shelter, good tides, and rock free mud for hulls to rest on. The River Medway is navigable upstream as far as Tonbridge, and empties into the Thames estuary at the Isle of Grain and Sheerness.

****

UPNOR CASTLE, Kent (right)

Upnor castle was built as a gun fort in 1559 to protect the naval harbour at Chatham. The only time its guns were fired in earnest was in 1667 when the Dutch raided the Medway. The Dutch sailed past the inefficient Upnor gunners almost unhindered to capture two British ships and set fire to several more. After this embarrassing failure, Upnor castle was converted into an ammunition store.

****

HISTORIC DOCKYARD
Chatham, Kent (right)

Four hundred years of history have been preserved at the Historic Dockyard, Chatham. Many naval vessels were built here: wooden sailing ships, such as Nelson's flagship Victory, right up to modern nuclear powered submarines. The Royal Navy left in 1984 bringing mass unemployment to the Medway towns. Britain's last World War II destroyer Cavalier, and the Victorian sloop Gannet, built at Sheerness in 1878, can both be seen here today, as well as the cold-war spy submarine Ocelot, launched in 1962.

****

ROCHESTER - CASTLE and CATHEDRAL
Kent (left)

The Romans built the first castle on this site to protect a bridge across the River Medway. Watling Street, the main Roman road from London to Dover crossed here. One of William the Conqueror's early motte and bailey castles was built on the same site. It was later converted to stone and the great tower was probably added during the 12th century. King John lay siege to the castle in 1215 and took it after two long months. He finally undermined the south-east tower and burned the props with the "fat of forty pigs" causing the tower to collapse. At the same time as the Normans built the castle, the cathedral was built by Bishop Gundolf who also designed the Tower of London. There have been many attacks on the cathedral. In the crypt, one of the finest in the country, there are graffiti thought to have been left by the soldiers of Simon de Montfort in 1264.

****

THE WYE CROWN

Kent (left & back cover)

Situated 1.5 km (1 mile) south-east of Wye, on the North Downs, the Wye Crown was designed in 1902 by T.J.Young who was at the time a lecturer at Wye College, for the coronation of King Edward VII in August of that year. It was carved in the chalk by students of the college, and lit on coronation night by 1,500 fairy lamps hung on notched sticks. It could be seen from as far away as Hastings. Each year there is a firework display at the site to celebrate Guy Fawkes. The crown hill figure is maintained by students at Wye College.

****

LEEDS CASTLE

Kent (above)

The castle takes its name from Ledian, a minister for Ethelbert IV, king of Kent, who lived here in the 9th century. The original Saxon manor house was enlarged by the Normans in 1119 to create the magnificent castle surrounded by an artificial lake. This was a royal castle from the time of Edward I to Henry VIII. The castle was used as a prison for Richard II, and later for the wife of Henry IV, and the aunt of Henry VI. After Henry VIII's death it was privately owned until 1974 when it was given to the nation.

****

BOXLEY AND THE PILGRIM'S WAY

Kent (above)

At the foot of the North Downs a string of villages marks the course of the medieval Pilgrim's Way, which led from Winchester to the shrine of Thomas Becket at Canterbury. Boxley, north of Maidstone, consists of just a few houses and a 13th century church, with pillars and arches made of chalk. In the Middle Ages, Boxley was known for its Cistercian Abbey, founded in 1146. Some ruins remain together with a magnificent tythe barn. The Downs are a haven for plants, especially orchids. Among the rich wildlife are the Adonis blue and the chalk hill blue, two butterfly species that depend on the chalk grassland for their survival.

****

CANTERBURY CATHEDRAL

Kent (left)

St Augustine came to Kent from Rome in AD597 to convert the Saxons to Christianity. Here in Canterbury he founded the mother church of the Anglican communion. In 1067 fire destroyed the Saxon cathedral and had to be rebuilt by the Normans. Just over a hundred years later, in 1170, knights acting for Henry II murdered the archbishop Thomas Becket in the cathedral. Henry II made a pilgrimage to Canterbury as a penance, and for the next 350 years, pilgrims came to pay their respects to Becket's shrine. They brought wealth and prosperity to the city, until Henry VIII brought it to an end. Next door to the cathedral lie the ruins of St Augustine's Abbey which was established around AD600. Many Saxon kings and early archbishops were buried here.

****

WALMER CASTLE, Kent (left)

Julius Caesar landed on the beach at Walmer in 55BC. Walmer Castle was built here for Henry VIII, with four large semi-circular bastions and a circular central tower. The castle's low walls provided less of a target and the battlements were rounded to deflect cannon balls. The moat was once filled by the sea at high tide. Since the 18th century, Walmer has been the official residence of the Lord Warden of the Cinque Ports, and its most famous occupant was the Duke of Wellington. Sir Winston Churchill, also Lord Warden, decided not to live there during the Second World War since it would have made him vulnerable to cross-Channel Nazi guns.

****

RICHBOROUGH CASTLE, Kent (above)

Just outside Sandwich, Richborough castle has some of the best preserved examples of Roman walls in England. They are massive, up to 4m thick and 8m high, and were built around AD287. The supply base and fort the Romans built defended Rutupiae, the chief port of entry for Roman legions. Watling Street, the great road that led to London and on to Chester, actually began at the west gate of the fort. The Roman emperor Claudius landed here in AD43 and built the original fortification. Later, in AD85, Agricola built a cruciform structure possibly to celebrate the final conquest of Britain. The cross rests on a platform covering an underground passage.

****

HEVER CASTLE
Kent (right)

Hever Castle is best known as the childhood home of Anne Boleyn. The oldest part of the castle was built in 1270, and consisted of a gatehouse with a walled bailey, a moat and a wooden drawbridge. The Bullen family acquired the castle in 1462, and later added a comfortable Tudor dwelling house. After attending the French Court, their daughter Anne changed her surname to Boleyn, and became lady-in-waiting to Henry VIII's first wife, Catherine. Henry frequently visited Hever to court Anne, finally marrying her in secret in 1533. The King was desperate for a son but Anne's only surviving child was the future Queen Elizabeth I. Henry became angry at the lack of a son, and had Anne arrested for High Treason based on false charges of adultery. Following her trial she was beheaded on 19th May 1536. Hever Castle slowly fell into disrepair until, in 1903, the American William Waldorf Astor set about restoring it, lavishing millions of dollars on it to recreate the treasure it is today.

****

CHARTWELL
Kent (left)

For more than forty years Chartwell was the much loved home of Sir Winston Churchill. The large house is set in hilly, wooded country to the south of Westerham, and today it is dedicated to Churchill's memory. The original house dated back to the 17th century and formed the base for the Victorian house which Churchill bought in 1922. Churchill added a new wing and made considerable alterations to the property, including the garden where he built walls with his own hands.

****

KNOLE HOUSE, Sevenoaks Kent (left)

Knole House is one of the largest and most famous homes in England. The present building dates from 1456 when it was used a palace for Archbishops of Canterbury, until Henry VIII took a fancy to it. It was inherited by Elizabeth I who presented it to her cousin, Thomas Sackville. Knole remained in the possession of the Sackville family until 1946 when it was handed over to the National Trust to preserve it for the nation.

****

BIGGIN HILL, Kent (below)

Situated on a plateau on top of the North Downs, Biggin Hill was perhaps the best known RAF fighter station for the Battle of Britain in 1940. By 1943, the station and its sector airfields were the first to claim a thousand enemy aircraft destroyed. The station was opened in January 1917 as a wireless testing park. Air to air, and air to ground telephony systems were also developed here. By 1924 the RAF had established itself at the airfield. Today, Biggin Hill is a growing airport for business aviation and is also a centre for flying training.

****

BRANDS HATCH, Kent (left)

The famous motor-racing circuit is located in a natural amphitheatre just 32 km (20 miles) from London, close to the M20 motorway. The circuit was established in the early 1920s when motorcycle events were held on grass tracks. After World War II a hard surface was introduced and many important British and international races, including the British Grand Prix, are now held here.

****

DUNGENESS, Kent (below)

Dungeness is a headland on the edge of Romney Marsh jutting out into the English Channel. This is the location for two nuclear power stations. It is also one of the world's largest expanses of shingle, the pattern of shingle ridges having built up over 5,000 years, with important geomorphology, plant and wildlife communities. Over 600 different types of plant are found here: a third of the species in the whole of Britain. Dungeness is one of the best places to find insects; some, such as the Sussex Emerald Moth are found nowhere else in Britain.

****

RAMSGATE, Kent (above)

When George IV visited Ramsgate in 1822, he raised its status by granting the title 'Royal Harbour'. This popular holiday resort boasts Georgian architecture and sandy beaches.

****

BROADSTAIRS, Kent (right)

Broadstairs, the "jewel in Thanet's crown" with its pleasant bays with sandy beaches, is a quiet town on the Kent coast between Margate and Ramsgate. The harbour and pier date from the time of Henry VIII and by the mid 19th century smuggling was rife. At that time Charles Dickens spent his summers here at Bleak House, which stands on a rise above the harbour.

****

FORENESS POINT, Kent (above)

Foreness Point is an excellent place to watch birds. Fulmars nest on the cliffs and skuas are sometimes attracted by the gulls flocking around the sewage pumping station's outfall in late summer. Waders such as purple sandpipers and a regular winter flock of great crested grebes are found here. Over the years birdwatchers have even spotted bittern, Cory's shearwater and gyrfalcon.

****

MARGATE, Kent (left)

Margate is the oldest and most famous seaside resort in Kent. Bathing machines were first used here: small caravans in which the bather changed into a bathing suit before being drawn into the water and could then emerge to swim, concealed from the gaze of others.

****

THE WHITE CLIFFS
Kent (right)

For centuries the famous white cliffs that extend eastwards from Brighton to Dover and beyond were a welcoming landmark to homeward bound soldiers and airmen in the two World Wars: never more so than for the Allied troops evacuated from Dunkirk in 1940. The cliffs form the northern boundary of the Strait of Dover which connects the North Sea with the English Channel and the Atlantic. The highest point is further west at Beachy Head (150m). Here as elsewhere, the cliffs are receding as the sea gradually erodes the soft chalk.

****

DOVER CASTLE
Kent (left)

The cliff-top castle that overlooks Dover harbour is one of the most impressive in Britain. It is built on the site of an Iron Age hill-fort and has been in constant use for over 800 years. Within its walls are two even older buildings: a 12m tower that formed the lower section of a Roman lighthouse built around AD45; and the Saxon church of St. Mary in Castro that still stands in all its original beauty. The fortifications at Dover were started by King Harold and continued by William the Conqueror after the Battle of Hastings in 1066. Henry II built a massive rectangular keep around 1180. King John extended the outer wall, and Henry III added an underground passage to an outwork on the northern side, so that surprise attacks could be made on a besieging army. The passage was extended during the Napoleonic wars, and the castle was further strengthened in the Second World War.

****

CHANNEL TUNNEL TERMINAL and CASTLE HILL FORT, Kent

The site of an Iron Age fort and 12th century earthworks on the **Castle Hill (left)** overlook the modern **Channel Tunnel terminus (above)** at Folkestone. The project to build the tunnel began in 1986. At the peak of its construction, 11 giant tunnel-boring machines, each costing up to £13 million and weighing 1,200 tons, chewed their way through the sub-aqueous chalk to produce two single-track railway tunnels flanking a narrower service tunnel. It took 150 electric and diesel locomotives to haul away the debris. The length of the tunnel (51km, 32 miles) required scrupulous safety measures. This undersea link between England and France ultimately cost £9 billion, and now carries some 500 train crossings each day.

****

SALTWOOD CASTLE, Hythe, Kent (above)

Saltwood Castle was originally built in AD488, probably on a Roman site, but was replaced in the 12th century by a Norman structure. Saltwood then became one of the south's strongest castles and the seat of the Warden of the Cinque Ports. The knights who murdered Thomas Becket stopped here to confer with Sir Ranulf de Broc on their way to Canterbury Cathedral to carry out Henry II's orders in 1170. Seriously damaged by an earthquake in 1580, Saltwood deteriorated into a ruin. Restoration work was carried out during the 19th and 20th centuries, and it is now privately owned.

****

THE ENGLISH CHANNEL (above)

The French call it "La Manche" (*The Sleeve*) in reference to its shape, an arm of the North Atlantic Ocean which gradually narrows towards the east to 34 km (21 miles) between Dover and Calais. Where the Strait is at its narrowest, the sea is very shallow; as little as 45 m deep, making possible the Channel Tunnel, a long dreamed about project which now speeds rail passengers between Britain and France. Historically the Channel, separating Britain from the Continent of Europe, has been a strategically important barrier to would-be invaders, but has also limited the range of species of fauna and flora present in the British Isles. Throughout much of the Pleistocene period, until about 20,000 years ago, Britain was connected to the Continent by dry land and it was only about 7,000 years ago that the sea level rose to sever that connection, isolating Britain from much of the northward migrations of species as the glaciers retreated at the end of the last ice age.

****

ARUNDEL CASTLE

West Sussex (next page, left)

A castle stood in this commanding position overlooking the Arun valley well before the Norman conquest. Parts of the present buildings date back to Norman times when the castle was part of the south coast defences. Henry II built the stone keep on the original motte in the 12th Century but little of that early structure remains. For more than 500 years, it has been the home of the Fitzalan family, earls of Arundel and, through marriage, the Howard family, dukes of Norfolk. The castle was damaged by Cromwell's cannons in the Civil War and became a ruin for almost 150 years, but was extensively rebuilt in the 18th and 19th centuries in Gothic style.

****

BODIAM CASTLE

West Sussex (next page, right)

Bodiam Castle was built by Sir Edward Dalyngrigge, a knight of Edward III's campaigns, who was granted a royal licence to fortify his house against possible invasion from France. Dalyngrigge actually built the castle afresh, some distance from his manor house, diverting a river to create an artificial lake around it. The castle's defences were tested only twice: it fell to a half-hearted attack by the Earl of Surrey in 1484, and again in the Civil War when the Parliamentary army threatened to bombard its walls using a new type of cannon. In 1917, Lord Curzon, the former Viceroy of India, restored the outer walls to their original medieval appearance.

****

SELSEY BILL, West Sussex (above)

In ancient times, Selsey was an island and it is still surrounded by water. On two sides the English Channel is held back by sea walls, while the brook of Broad Rife runs to the north-west and Pagham harbour lies to the north. However this large inlet is now effectively cut off from the sea. There was a Roman settlement here called Regnum but there is little of pre-Norman Selsey left, for the sea engulfed it long ago.

****

BOGNOR REGIS, West Sussex (left)

Bognor is reputed to be one of the sunniest places in England, and was one of the early fashionable bathing places for royalty in the late 18th century. Queen Victoria was especially fond of it. Like many of the south coast resorts, Bognor developed from an inland village, in this case South Bersted, when Sir Richard Hotham bought up vast areas of coastal land for development. In the 19th century there were no sea walls to protect the resort from storms and, as a result, parts of old Bognor were washed away, including a military barracks used during the Napoleonic wars.

****

CHICHESTER HARBOUR
West Sussex (left)

South of Chichester, cathedral city and county town of West Sussex, the deep inlet of Chichester channel provides a safe haven for sailing craft. The channel feeds Chichester Harbour, England's biggest inland harbour with over 88 kilometres (55 miles) of coastline. This is the heart of British yachting, a world of deep cut creeks and mudflats where yachts decorate the water like flocks of sea birds.

****

NEWHAVEN, East Sussex (below)

During World War I, Newhaven harbour was the main military supply port for the British Expeditionary Force in France, and the area was well defended. August 1942 saw Newhaven play a major part in the ill-fated Dieppe raid. Some 5,000 troops and heavy equipment departed, but only 1,400 men returned. Coastal fortifications near Newhaven can be traced back a thousand years before William the Conqueror's invasion fleet sailed into Pevensey Bay in 1066. But the fort that exists today was built in 1862 to deter invasion by the French. The threat is long gone – Newhaven now offers a car ferry service to Dieppe.

****

BRIGHTON, East Sussex (above and right)

Brighton's marina (above) lies less than a kilometre from the centre. It is protected by two giant breakwaters made up of 100 massive caissons, each equivalent in height to a four-storey house. The area enclosed totals over 50 hectares with berths for up to 1300 boats.

The fantastic seaside palace, **the Royal Pavilion (right)** with its Indian domes and minarets and its Chinese style interior, has become a landmark not to be missed. The Pavilion is the fruit of the vivid imagination of the Prince Regent, later George IV, and his collaboration with the architect John Nash. Today some of the finest examples of Regency architecture in England can be seen in Brighton and Hove.

WHITE CLIFFS, East Sussex (above)

Stretching westwards from Beachy Head is a long line of chalk cliffs, their shape earning them the name the Seven Sisters. They lie between Birling Gap and Cuckmere Haven, popular landing places for smugglers in the 18th and 19th centuries.

****

BEACHY HEAD, East Sussex (left)

The spectacular chalk cliffs of Beachy Head, 150m high, are the seaward extension of the South Downs. Facing southward, they face the force of south-westerly gales, which have through the ages eroded the soft chalk in the shape of isolated stacks. At one time there were seven of these, known as the Charleses, but they have all disappeared – the last fell in 1875. A lighthouse protects shipping from the dangerous shallow waters with its swirling surf.

****

CABURN HILL FORT, East Sussex (above)

Before it was settled, Caburn Hill was covered by dense woodland, probably yew. This isolated part of the beautiful rolling landscape of the South Downs overlooks the River Ouse and the town of Lewes. It is the site of an early Iron Age fort, with earth walls that would have been topped by a stockade. It was in use from about 500BC to the beginning of the Roman occupation in AD100. The first settlers were of the European Halstatt culture, but the hill fort was later taken over by newcomers from La Tène culture. Weaving combs made from deer antler and perforated chalk weaving blocks for keeping threads taut have been found here. A lead weight was also found, thought to be similar to the Celtic standard unit of measure, suggesting trade with outsiders.

****

LONG MAN OF WILMINGTON, East Sussex (right)

The recent discovery of a drawing of the Long Man dating from 1710 is currently the earliest record of this enigmatic hill figure. It may be much older however. Today, the Long Man exists in outline only, naked and featureless; but this may not always have been so. Ancient hill figures are known to have been altered in shape, features and even size over the centuries. Among British hill figure giants though, the Long Man is the biggest, measuring 70m from head to toe. But he is out of proportion, almost twice as tall as a correctly proportioned figure. Some say that this is so that the figure can be understood from the low ground to the north, from where the perspective is changed considerably. In fact the proportions seem more correct when viewed from the air.

****

HASTINGS, East Sussex (left)

After landing with his army at Pevensey William the Conqueror made preparations here for the Battle of Hastings, which was fought 9.5 km (6 miles) to the north-west at Battle (right). The town later became one of the Cinque Ports and prospered during the Middle Ages, but suffered from raids by the French during the Hundred Years War. The harbour eventually silted up but, during the 19th century, the town became a popular bathing resort.

****

BATTLE ABBEY, East Sussex (right)

The town of Battle was built on the site of the momentous Battle of Hastings in 1066, when King Harold was defeated by William the Conqueror. On the day of the battle William vowed that if he was victorious, he would build an abbey there. The terrace of the abbey marks the point on Seniac Hill where the English army took up their positions. It overlooks a gulley where the Norman army stood. Attacking the English uphill put the Normans at a disadvantage. But as the Normans retreated the English abandoned their advantageous position to pursue them. The Normans rallied and destroyed the English. Harold was killed by Norman knights on Seniac Hill, and William became king of England.

****

BEWL WATER and THE WEALD

East Sussex (right)

Bewl Water is a manmade reservoir on the border of Kent and East Sussex, south-east of Tunbridge Wells.

****

EPSOM RACECOURSE
Surrey (left)

The grandstand at the famous Epsom racecourse was built in 1927, the first ever to be made of reinforced concrete. It is said that in Cromwell's time, Royalists would hold race meetings here on the Downs as an excuse for a gathering. But Epsom racecourse began in earnest towards the end of the 18th century when the Earl of Derby founded the famous race that still bears his name.

****

GOLF COURSE AT WOODCOTE PARK
Surrey (below)

****

M25/M23 JUNCTION
Surrey (left)

Drivers have voted the traffic-clogged London orbital motorway, the M25, their favourite stretch of road. The jam-infested 190km (119 miles) road came top of the motorway league in a national survey. Many drivers took a light-hearted view of the regular heavy congestion. One described the M25 as "the only free car park in the capital". Another reckoned it was "one of the most peaceful roads in the world – the only place you get the chance to relax and watch the world (not) go by".

****

NEW MALDEN, Surrey (above)

The fringe of London at New Malden, with the A3, one of the main arteries for traffic into the city.

****

SHERE, Surrey (left)

Shere is one of the prettiest of Surrey's villages, with weeping willows, narrow streets and old cottages bent and twisted with age. The old Norman church has changed little in 600 years.

****

DORKING, Surrey (right)

Dorking, situated close to Box Hill and the north Downs, is an ancient market town which is expanding to accommodate an increasing population of residents who travel to work in London.

****

BOX HILL, Surrey (left)

One of the best known beauty spots in the south-east, Box Hill on the North Downs rises to 183m. The site is a mixture of woodland and chalk grassland, and is now owned by the National Trust. The hill is named after the box trees which are native to the site. These support a rare insect, the box shield bug. As well as box there are lots of yew trees, beeches and oaks. Many orchids grow on the grassland and over two-thirds of British butterfly species have been recorded here.

****

GUILDFORD CATHEDRAL
Surrey (left)

Guildford's Cathedral of the Holy Spirit was the first to be built on an entirely new site since the time of Henry VIII's Reformation. The foundation stone rests on stones from Canterbury and Winchester cathedrals. It was laid in 1936 but building was halted during World War II. The cathedral was finally completed in 1961. A settlement was first recorded at Guildford in the time of Alfred the Great. An Anglo-Saxon fortification was built on a partly artificial mound, then after the Norman Conquest a stone castle was built which became a popular Royal residence during the Middle Ages, when Guildford's wool industry thrived. Today only part of the castle's keep remains as a ruin.

****

COMPTON AND HOG'S BACK
Surrey (right)

Compton is an ancient village just below the long ridge of Hog's Back. There are five magnificent Cedar of Lebanon trees here, among the biggest and oldest in the country. The very fine church is Norman and the tower dates from Saxon times. Pilgrims passed by Compton on their way from Winchester to Becket's shrine at Canterbury.

****

FARNHAM CASTLE
Surrey (right)

In the 12th century, Henry of Blois, Bishop of Winchester, built a wooden castle on the road from Winchester to London. During the 13th century, it was rebuilt in stone and a chapel was added. By 1475 the large brick entry tower was built. Both Henry VII and Henry VIII stayed here, and it was used as a base for hunting expeditions by James I. During the Civil War, it was a Royalist stronghold until December 1642, when it was taken by Parliamentary forces and used as a prison for those loyal to the king. Restorations were undertaken during the 18th and 19th centuries, and from 1927 to 1955 it was the home of the bishops of Guildford.

****

NEWARK PRIORY
Surrey (left)

Newark Priory was founded in 1189 by Ruald de Clane and his wife Beatrice of Send, and dedicated to the Virgin Mary and Thomas Becket. When Henry VIII dissolved the monasteries in 1537, valuables were sent to the Tower of London and the land given to the Master of the King's Horse. It has been said that a cannon was employed from the top of Church Hill to bombard and demolish the priory. The dissolution of Newark was hard on local people, as the land was then taken by the King for his hunting park that stretched all the way to Hampton Court.

****

LAST REFUGE Ltd

Nature is a precious inheritance, to be cared for and cherished by all of us. Last Refuge Ltd is a small company primarily dedicated to documenting and archiving endangered environments and species in our rapidly changing world, through films, images and research. The company was established in 1992, while studying wild giant pandas in the Qinling mountains of central China, which seemed, literally, to be the "last refuge" for these charismatic animals. The company's name was adopted for that project and it seemed logical to continue with it, embracing new projects worldwide. Two films on lemurs in Madagascar quickly followed and the ring-tailed lemur became the company's logo. Adrian Warren and Dae Sasitorn, who run the company out of a farmhouse in Somerset, have created a special web site, www.lastrefuge.co.uk, in order to present their work, which is becoming a huge resource for information, and an extensive photographic archive of still and moving images for both education and media. Ultimately they hope to offer special conservation awards to fund work by others.

ADRIAN WARREN

Adrian Warren is a biologist, and a commercial pilot, with over thirty years experience as a photographer and filmmaker, working worldwide for the BBC Natural History Unit, and as a director in the IMAX giant screen format. He has recently designed a new wing mount camera system for aircraft to further develop his interest in aviation, aerial filming and photography. As a stills photographer, he has a personal photographic archive of over 100,000 pictures, with worldwide coverage of wildlife, landscapes, aerials, and peoples. His photographs appear in books, magazines, advertisements, posters, calendars, greetings cards and many other products. His awards include a Winston Churchill Fellowship; the Cherry Kearton Medal from the Royal Geographical Society in London; the Genesis award from the Ark Trust for Conservation; an International Prime Time Emmy; and the Golden Eagle Award from New York.

DAE SASITORN

Dae Sasitorn is an academic from the world of chemistry but has given it up to follow her love for nature. She manages the company and has created and designed the Last Refuge website as well as scanning thousands of images for the archive. She has also become a first-class photographer in her own right.

THE PHOTOGRAPHY

Adrian and Dae operate their own Cessna 182G out of a tiny farm strip close to their house. They bought the single engined four-seater aircraft in May 1999 in order to develop a new wing mounted camera system for cinematography. The 1964 Cessna was in beautiful condition, and had only one previous owner. It is the perfect aircraft for aerial work: small, manoeuvrable, with plenty of power, and the high wing configuration offering an almost unrestricted view on the world below. With twenty degrees of flap it is possible to fly as slowly as sixty knots. The cabin side window opens upwards and outwards and is kept open by the air flow. Over London, however, where it is not permitted to fly a single engine fixed wing aircraft in case of engine failure, the Cessna had to be abandoned in favour of a helicopter equipped with floats.

The photographs were taken on Hasselblad medium format 6x6cm cameras and lenses (mostly 50mm) using Fujichrome Velvia film. Waiting for the right weather, with a clear atmosphere and less than fifty per cent cloud cover, required being on standby for months.

First Published in 2003 by Myriad Books Limited,
35 Bishopsthorpe Road, London, SE26

ISBN 1 904154 43 3

Designed by Dae Sasitorn and Adrian Warren
Last Refuge Limited
Printed in China